Just Say "YES" to

Laughing
Your Way
To
Fitness
With
Yoga And Meditation
(and that's no joke)

Sushil Bhatia

THE LAUGHING CLUBS OF AMERICA.

Sushil Bhatia
Laughing Clubs Of America
C/o JMD,
59 Fountain Street, Framingham,
MA 01702 (U.S.A.)
Tel: (508) 620-6563
1-800-752-5563
Fax:(508) 620-7563

Laughing

Your Way
To
Fitness
With
Yoga   And Meditation
(and that's no joke)

Sushil Bhatia
Illustrations by Pat Woodward and Sushil Bhatia

To
My Wife

Urvashi

For all your help and encouragement

Meditatively Yours,

Sushil

(his mark)

OM

OM is the eternal, imperishable symbol.
OM is the universe, and this is the exposition of OM.
The Past, the present and the future: all that was, all that is, all that
will be, is OM.
Likewise, all that may exist beyond the bounds of time- that too is OM.

PREFACE

Good health is our greatest asset. However, with the current hectic pace of life and the high pressure living, we all suffer from varying degrees of stress. Stress and tension disrupt life and affect emotions, showing up in the form of fatigue, poor health and a lack of inner serenity.

To maintain good health, it is necessary to know how to deal with stress. But, first we need to know what causes stress. This book explains these causes and demonstrates the technique "How to Stay Fit and Stress – FREE.the EASY WAY" through Yoga and Meditation.

We've also included segments on the value and art of laughter and the use of Yoga and common sense to overcome problems of sleeplessness…all-important in maintaining a good health program.

It is especially useful for people who are busy with their professions, families and other commitments and who don't have the time to go to health clubs or other places to exercise. These simple exercises are aimed at three of the most common problems: tension, sinus headaches, backaches and digestion related difficulties.

The greatest advantage of these exercises is that they can be done anywhere, and no special equipment or set up is needed.

We have purposely designed our book in a compact easy – to –read, illustrated format so that people on the go can fit the exercise routine into their busy schedules.

We hope that you will find that by regularly practicing the techniques we've described, you will enjoy the benefits of a fit and stress-free life.

Sushil Bhatia

ACKNOWLEDGEMENTS
and
THANKS

Acknowledgements cannot even start without thanking Pat Woodward and Kenyi Parada. Both of them have very patiently out up with the changing requirements of the sketches and the script. Pat repeatedly came up with innovative cartoons to show the poses and the exercises. Her sketches are better than my explanations. Kenyi, with a great deal of patience, deciphered my handwriting and printed out many, many versions of the script. Both kept on laughing as they worked through the revisions. Thank you both so much.

I must thank Kirit Shandilya in Mumbai, India who insisted I learn Yoga from his teacher Mahavir Ji. Thanks to his Persistence, I gave in and my life changed for the better – forever.

There are so may others who have helped me over the years and who have urged me to teach Yoga and Meditation. Nammi Chander, Sonia Saxena, Dr. Ishwar Sharma and Neelu Sharma were the first ones to convince me to start Yoga classes. Not only did they assemble the groups, but also provide the place to conduct classes when no other place was available. Thanks to all of you.

More recently, Brinda Shah and Punita Khatau have effectively been promoting the Laughing Clubs of America. I am most grateful.

I am also grateful to the Town of Framingham, Jim Egan and Sam Swisher for recognizing the potential of Laughter Therapy and for providing space at the town hall for the Laughter Therapy meetings.

To Nupur Kohli, Harish Dang and Arsh Mehrota, I send thanks for promoting the Laughter Therapy, Yoga and Meditation sessions on the radio programs "Jhaankar and Sounds of India and the TV program " Aap ka Manoranjan" respectively.

Thanks also to Ted Welte, Rutty Guzdar, Peter Ten Broeck, Dr. C. B. S. Patel, Dr. Sanjeev Sharma and many others who have supported and encouraged me over the years.

Thanks to Jiten Saxena for being a good friend and for being there whenever I needed to chat.

Extra and special thanks to Bharat Khatau for very useful and fruitful discussions on business, spirituality and the essence of Geetha and for making those morning walks so interesting and stimulating. Something I looked forward to every weekend. Really appreciate those walks followed by '**chai and chat**'.

And lastly, my b.i..gg..e.s.t thanks to my in house cheerleaders: my <u>favorite</u> wife URVASHI and my children- Mishi, Kriti and Divi – who have helped me keep my sense of humor sharp and have kept laughing at my jokes… even my non- jokes!

Laughingly

Sushil Bhatia

LAUGHING YOUR WAY TO FITNESS

And that's no joke

Stress and tension disrupt life and emotions showing up in the form of fatigue, poor health and lack of inner serenity.

People use a number of techniques to relax and stay fit. One of these is an ancient technique called **Laughter Therapy.**

The feeling of joy that one experiences while laughing is unique and unparalleled. This, combined with Yoga and Meditation, harmonizes all our sense organs in a moment of total concentration and brings equilibrium to mind, body and breathing.... Which are like three strands of a rope.

It has been proven by researchers all over the world that laughter is a simpler, easier and more enjoyable form of stress busting than any of the more sophisticated and expensive methods.

In spite of its benefits, it has not always been possible for most people, from those working long hours in the field to those in high –powered professional positions, to practice laughter therapy on a daily basis because of the ongoing stress in their lives. Most people need some stimulus to provoke laughter.... Jokes or funny experiences to really set them off.

Under this program, folks are invited to join in-group laughter, which builds up without relying on specific jokes or constructed humorous events, for 15-20 minutes in every session. This is followed by breathing and other exercise for fitness and relaxation.

Participants have found this technique to be very relaxing, and have experienced dramatic relief from stress-related disorders such as sleeplessness, anxiety, depression, tension and migraine headaches, hypertension, chronic bronchitis, asthma and a host of other ailments.

The Exercise last about 30-45 minutes, require no equipment other than a sheet or beach towel and are generally done in a group of between 2 and 20.

but, first, this...............

Laugh Your Head Off

1. A 10 second belly laugh is as good as three minutes on a rowing machine

2. Laughing helps to relax. After laughing, the pulse and heart rate decrease to below normal causing a feeling of relaxation that can last up to 45 minutes

3. Laughter reduces pain by stimulating endorphins. the pleasure-giving chemicals in the body. Endorphins allow temporary relief of pain and negative emotions which are directly related to illness.

4. Laughter triggers certain chemicals that cause the immune system to kick in

5. Laughing helps with chronic breathing problems by aiding ventilation and clearing mucus.

6. Joy of laughing brings relaxation, conquers stress and reduces pain

7. Laughter creates positive and, with relaxation, helps the body to function better.

8. Laughter stimulates the brain as well as the body.

9. With laughter, not only do the facial muscles get a good workout, but the cardiovascular system does also due to the increase in pulse, breathing and circulation.

10. Laughter stimulates the brain with greater alertness, which can enhance memory and sociability thereby linking wit and wisdom.

Keep on Laughing ……..Seriously !

Laughter and
the Art of Laughter

To keep the body healthy, it is necessary to laugh! "Laughter is the best medicine" is a saying, which has been heard by almost everyone repeatedly.

A hearty laugh relieves the tension from the body and helps overcome fatigue and tiredness. With laughter, the body feels rejuvenated, anger subsides and the mind is ready to face new tasks.

As with anything else, laughter – or the art of laughing has different forms:

1. **ROLLING WITH LAUGHTER**
Laugh heartily and freely with no restraints
whatsoever while rolling the
upper part of the body

BENEFITS
Relieves tension and stress – relaxes the body.
Opens and closes the lungs and the chest. Stomach gets exercised and intestines become stronger. Eyesight also improves.

2. **MEEK LAUGHTER**
Laugh heartily but without opening the mouth
And without making any sound.
Feel as if all the parts are participating in laughter.

BENEFITS
This exercise benefits the intestines
And digestion by releasing stress from the body.

3. **QUIET LAUGHTER**
Laugh heartily with the mouth open,
But making no sound at all.

BENEFITS
Relaxes the body, benefits the digestive system.
Also helps to relieve the digestive system.

4. COCKTAIL LAUGHTER

As the name implies this laughter is a mixture of many different types of laughters an that is why it is called cocktail laughter.
 While shaking hands with other people in the group and looking into their eyes   you make the sounds "
 HA..HA….HA….HA., HO…..HO… HO….HO….HO…, HEE. HEE…HEE, HEE. HEY…, HEY…, HEY…, HEY…..

BENEFITS: Helps overcome shyness, inhibitions and breaks barriers with other people. Massages facial muscels, provides a feeling of lightness, relief and enjoyment

HOW TO STAY FIT AND STRESS FREE

.......the EASY WAY

In order to enjoy the benefits of good health through the reduction of stress in our lives, we first need to understand what causes stress.

When an emotional upheaval takes places – like the loss of a loved one, bad news, conflict with one's boss or missed deadlines at work- an alarm goes off in the brain. This triggers the endocrine system of the body, which reacts to the stressor. The glands then produce adrenaline for a "fight or flight" response.

Action taken immediately reduces this stress and tension. Inaction prolongs the state of stress resulting in exhaustion, the body's defenses becoming weak resulting in headaches, backaches and a lot of other physical and emotional problems including depression.

There are many ways of dealing with stress and tension. Most physical exercise programs build up certain parts of the body can waste a lot of energy, and the practitioner can end up exhausted very quickly. When not handled properly, lopsided development of the body can result. *It is essential that whatever exercises are adopted should provide good balanced results and harmony to the mind body and breathing.*

One of the most effective and well-regarded methods of bringing harmony to the body is through the practice of Yoga and Meditation. Most people believe that doing yoga means either standing on your head or forming your body in pretzel-like shapes. Many think that meditation is sitting on the floor chanting "mantras" while the body sways from side to side. It is important to clear up these misconceptions.

Yoga is the study of harmony – harmony of the mind, body and life force (breathing). These three functions are like the three strands of a rope. They support each other. Neither one of them can exist without the other. Like the universe, our personality consists of three forms: static or inert (Body), dynamic (breathing) and the life force, which transcends the other two (Mind).

Harmony among these three keeps us in good physical and mental shape while disharmony results in problems. The **balance** between these three makes our personality-especially a happy one.

GOOD BALANCE – MIND, BODY and BREATHING

HAPPY PERSONALITY

If these three things of our personality – mind, breathing and body - are not in harmony, the results make us unhappy, cranky and irritable.

OFF BALANCE – MIND, BODY and BREATHING

UN......HAPPY...... PERSONALITY

Yoga teaches us how to bring about this harmony by prescribing postures (Asanas) for the body, synchronizing it with breathing for life force (and energy) and relaxation techniques for mind control (Meditation). Yoga exercises are not tiring. They make the body supple and they conserve energy. Regular practice of Yoga helps the body to reach a state of equilibrium, provides more energy, builds up resistance to disease and results in a healthier body.

Yoga is believed to be the destroyer of pain. Proper Yoga exercises provide self – healing effects and has been used to provide relief to people suffering from dyspepsia, backaches, headaches, and sinus problems, soothe hunger. Above all, they bring serenity of mind through stress reduction.

Regular practice of Yoga also improves memory and concentration and generates a feeling of general well being.

Through Yoga and Meditation, the practitioner learns relaxation techniques and how to cope successfully with everyday situations of stress and tensions. The greatest benefits of these exercises are that they are portable. They can be done anywhere: in the home, office, on an airplane, in hotel rooms, even while waiting for an appointment. No special equipment or set up is necessary for these easy techniques.

PREPARING YOURSELVES FOR EXERCISES AND MEDITATION

1. The best time to practice these exercises is in the morning

2. Do not wear spectacles or loose ornaments when doing exercises

3. Wear loose clothing

4. Exercises preferably should be done in the morning and on an empty stomach or at least a half hour before meal.

5. Tea, coffee or a light snack can be taken 15 minutes after exercising- or, if need be, at least a half hour before

6. After the exercises, practice meditation for 20 minutes.

7. If it is not possible to practice all the Asanas (postures) in the morning, you can do some at night or divide them into two segments on alternate days.

8. Before starting, make sure the room is clear and airy.

9. Regularity is the most important if you want to derive the full benefit from these exercises

10. Do not allow your mind to wander during the exercises. Ignore all disturbances and distractions. Focus on what you are doing.

11. Never do the exercise in a violent, jerky or forced manner. They should be done in an effortless, slow, steady, relaxed and graceful manner.

12. It is not necessary to reach the perfect position of an exercise as shown in the drawings.

13. Do not overdo. Take your personal capacity into account. You can slowly build up.

14. Do not mix any other form of exercise with Yoga.

15. With the exercises done correctly, you will emerge from a yoga session feeling light   refreshed and cheerful.

16. Do SAVASANA for about 10 minutes whenever you feel tired or exhausted.

17.   Start and conclude your daily sessions with a calm, serene and pleasant frame of mind, and above all, an attitude of devotion.

18.   Do exercises in a systematic step-by-step manner. For them to be effective, you must not be in a hurry.

19.   To reap the maximum benefits, avoid habits harmful to health and lead a hygienic life. Observe moderation and maintain a healthy balance in food, sleep, work and pleasures throughout your daily life.

"Yoga becomes the destroyer of sorrows and miseries for him who is moderate in eating, pleasures, work, sleep and other daily affairs"
Geeta: VI: 17

Yoga and Meditation Exercises

SITTING POSTURES

Either of the Following sitting postures can be used for the practice of Yoga and Meditation. The selection depends upon the practitioner and his or her body condition when starting, and what is most convenient.

- Padamasana……. (Lotus Position)
- Sukhasana……….(Easy Posture: i.e., sitting crosslegged

Sukhasana is the easier of the two and more popular with beginners.

PADMASANA (LOTUS POSITION)

Sit erect with legs stretched foreward (Fig. 1). Bend right leg, and place the right foot on the left thigh. Join the Head of the right foot against the left groin (Fig 2). Similarly, Place the left foot on the right thigh and press the heal against the right groin. (Fig. 2).
Place the hands on the knees, stretch the palms fully, and join the tip of the index fingers with the thumb of each respective hand. (Fig. 3)

This is the proper PADMASANA or LOTUS POSITION

Fig. 1   Fig. 2   Fig. 3

SUKHASANA (EASY POSTURE)

Sit Erect with legs stretched forward. Bend legs one after the other at the knees so that the feet are next to the hips, i.e., sit cross-legged.
You don't have to place them on top of the thighs.
The Position of the hands and the fingers is the same as the lotus Position
This is the proper SUKHANSANA or easy posture.

TECHNIQUE

Sit in either of these postures. Close your eyes. Breath normally. Focus on the sound of your breathing. Stay in this position for 10 minutes.

BENEFITS:

These traditional sitting postures provide: physical and mental stability. They calm and ton the nervous system and remove restlessness, anxiety and fear. They relieve the stiffness of ankles, legs, knee joints, and guard against arthritis and rheumatism. They also strengthen the back muscles and conserve vital energy.

EXERCISES

The Following YOGA exercises should take approximately 25 minutes doing each 5-10 times, with about 20 minutes more for meditation.

FINGER POWER

The five fingers of the hand represent the five elements of the Universe:

- Thumb (1)   Fire
- Forefinger (2) Air
- Middle Finger (3)   Sky
- Finger (4)   Earth
- Finger (5)   Water

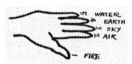

EXERCISE 1: EASY BREATHING

Sit on the floor in Lotus Position or Easy Posture.

- **Position A**
  Make a circle with thumb (1) and
  Forefinger (2) touching each other.
  Place hands with palms open and
  facing up, with other fingers out
  stretched on the knees.

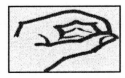

BENEFITS: Relaxation, mental peace, good concentration, good memory and sound sleep.

- **Position B:**
  Thumb (1) and fingers (3&4) touching.
  Breath normally as in Position A.
  BENEFITS: Aids in acid indigestion and
  removing contaminants from the system.

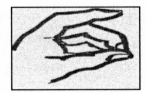

Position C
Thumb (1) and fingers (4& 5) touching. Breath
normally as in position A

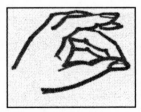

BENEFITS: Eliminates fatigue. Provides more
life force and energy.

THREE MOST IMPORTANT THINGS

*BREATHING

      *BREATHING

            *BREATHING

THE POWER OF PROPER

BREATHING

EXERCISE 2: OM

Sit in the same position as in Exercise 1,
Position A. breathe in. Hold Form " O "
with the lips, and make sound " O "
 while exhaling through the
lips until 2/3 of
your breadth is exhaled. End with the
 sound "m..m..m".
Repeat five times.

BENEFITS: Relaxes the mind, improves
concentration and provides vital energy.

EXERCISE 3: COUNT OF "15"

Sit in a LOTUS Position/Easy Posture.

- **Position A**
  With Thumb (1) and forefinger (2) touching,
  and other fingers outstretched, put hands
  with palms upside down on the knees.
  Breathe in for a count of 5.
  Hold for a count of 7. Count 1 and start again.
  Total count = 15.

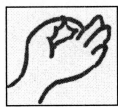

- **Position B**
  Have thumb and forefinger (2) still touching
  with other fingers closed towards the palm –
  put hands upside down on the knees.
  Repeat breathing to count of
  15 as above.

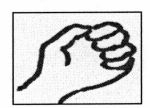

- **Position C**
  Bend the thumb so that it is touching the base
  of the little finger (5). Close fingers on the top
  of the thumb (both Hands)
  Place closed hands upside down on the knees
  (as in Position A above).
  Repeat breathing to the count of 15.
  As you practice this, make sure the elbows are bent when the hands are
  resting on the knees. This exercise can also be done sitting in a chair. In
  that case, place your hands /palms on your thighs instead of the knees, this
  assures that your arms are bent at the elbows.

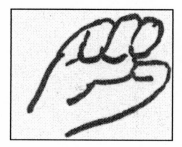

BENEFITS: Position A: tones up the digestive system and improves the
functions of organs in the abdominal cavities.
Position B: benefits the heart, lungs, hands and shoulders.
Position C: gets rid of headaches, clears sinuses and relieves pain due to
congestion in the wind cavities connecting the ears.

EXERCISE 4: ALTERNATE BREATHING

This exercise consists of:
a.   Slowly inhaling through the left nostril, then slowly exhaling through the right nostril.
b.   Slowly inhaling through the right nostril then slowly exhaling through the left nostril.
      Ratio of in to out is 1-2 (e.g. 5 seconds in, 10 seconds out).

TECHNIQUE
Sit in the Lotus Position or easy posture – or sit erectly in a chair.
a.   Close the right nostril with your thumb. Slowly inhale through left nostril. Now remove thumb from the right nostril, and with the forefinger, close the left nostril, and with the forefinger, close the left nostril. Exhale through the right nostril
   .

b.   When the air is out, inhale through the right nostril slowly. Now close the right nostril with the thumb remove the forefinger from the left nostril and exhale slowly through the left nostril.

In the beginning, the time ratio for in and out breathing should be 1-2 (e.g., in to the count of 5, and exhale to the count of 10). Count mentally only.
BENEFITS: Feeling of freshness, more energy and lightness of mind and body. Purifies blood and increases resistance to disease. Steadies the mind in concentration. Improves digestion and appetite.

EXERCISE 5

After 4-5 weeks of doing the above, you may introduce holding of the breathe for in – hold-out:, 1-2-2 ratio. If you have difficulty with "hold", practice only alternate breathing.
BENEFITS: Same as above.

EXERCISE 6: SITALL (Cooling feeling)

Sit in Lotus Position or Easy Posture. Or in a chair. Sit erect.
Form an "O" with the lips. Place the tongue on the lower lip.
Breathe in through the mouth and hold. Relax the tongue and
close the mouth. Lower your head, and touch chin to the chest.
Keep head down for about 15 seconds. Lift head and breathe out
through the nose. After some practice, you should feel a " cooling"
effect – a relaxed feeling.
BENEFITS: Cools the system, soothes the eyes and ears and purifies
the blood. Quenches thirst and appeases hunger. Cures indigestion.

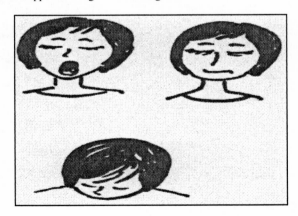

EXERCISE 7: BHRRUMARI (Bee sound)

Sit in Lotus Position or Easy Posture on the floor –or in a chair sitting erectly.

Block ears with fingers and breathe in through the nose.
Fold tongue inwards to touch the roof of the mouth. Close
your eyes and make a sound
like a bee while slowly breathing out through the nose.
Repeat 5 times.
BENEFITS: Clears sinus and head congestion. Excellent to help relive symptoms of
head colds or allergies.

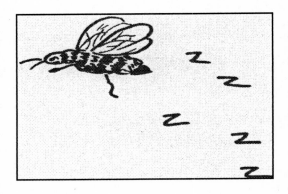

EXERCISE 8: VAJRASANA

Stand on your knees. Separate the heels apart, and
join the big toes together at the center.
Sit down firmly in between the two heels.
Place the hands upside down on the knees.
Eyes closed, feel the cool air touching the nostrils
as it enters during inhaling then the warm air moving
out during exhalation.
Sit tall, erect and effortless for 3-5 minutes while breathing normally. At the end
of 3-5 minutes slowly stand up.

BENEFITS: Improves digestion, relieves flatulence, mobilizes stiff ankles and
knees, and is useful for case of varicose veins.

EXERCISE 9: UP –STRECTHED ARMS
Stand Straight with feet slightly apart (6-8 inches).

While breathing in and rising on toes, stretch arms up
over the head to a clap position. Hold breath and turn palms
out. Bring arms down slowly while breathing out and coming
back down to the starting position.

BENEFITS: This exercise improves posture and balance,
 increases physical and mental poise, exercises the lungs
and strengthens the wrists, calves and feet. It also firms and tones
 the muscles of the arms shoulders, chest back, abdomen hips and legs.

EXERCISE 10: TIP TOE SQUATING

Stand in the same position as the above exercise
with feet slightly apart
While breathing in, hold arms straight out in front,
palms facing down, parallel to the floor and back straight.
Come up on toes. Focus on an object in front of you.
Keeping back straight, come down to "sit on heels"
while remaining on toes. Hold. Lower arms to side and
heels to floor while breathing out.

BENEFITS: This improves balance and posture while
limbering and strengthening the feet, knees and thighs.

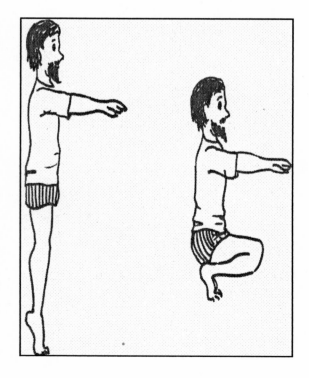

EXERCISE 11: BACKWARD BEND AND FORWARD BEND STRETCHING

Stand straight with feet about 12 inches apart.
Bend slowly forward and let palms touch knees. Breath out. While breathing in, bring arms up overhead stretching back as far as you can.
Star breathing out and slowly bend down to touch toes for 30 seconds. Bring arms up and stretch while breathing in. Bring arms to side breathing out.

BENEFITS: regular practice brings increased suppleness. The nervous system is toned, the spine stretched and limbered, the abdominal organs are massaged, the legs firmed and toned and the hamstrings at the backs of the thighs loosened. The facial tissues and scalp are nourished with an additional supply of blood.

EXERCISE 12 STRETCHES AND TWIST

Stand erect with feet 12" –18" apart for good balance.

Breathe in and raise arms shoulder high and parallel to
the ground. Pick an object behind you to focus on. As you
swing around to see the object, breathe out. On return to the
front, breathe in. Breathe out as you swing in the opposite
direction, and breathe in as you return to the front. Always
keep arms at shoulder height. Continue for about 5 times for
 each direction.

BENEFITS: Same as in Exercise 11.

EXERCISE 13: COBRA POSE

Lie down on the chest and stomach full length.

Put palms next to the shoulders. Keeping elbows close to the body, raise yourself from waist up while breathing in. Hold this position for 30 seconds while focusing on an object in front of you.
Slowly come down while breathing out.

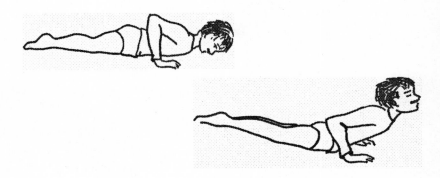

BENEFITS: During these exercises the muscles at the back come into play. The pressure is exerted on the vertebrae from the neck down to the lower part of the spinal column, which gets toned up due to the copious supply of blood becoming available to this region during practice. This exercise soothes backaches, renders the spinal column more flexible and keeps it in good health. It also has a beneficial effect on the kidneys (adrenal glands) and stimulates digestion.

NOTE: People with a stiff spinal column should start slowly and carefully. Sudden movements should be avoided.

EXERCISE 14: MAGARASANA (Relaxing)

Lie on chest and stomach.

Bend arm and put hands one on top of the other and parallel to the shoulders (palms on the floor). Rest head facing on the hands. Spread the legs slightly apart with feet pointing outwards. Breathe normally and RELAX..

BENEFITS: Relaxes the mind and the body. Relieves tension.

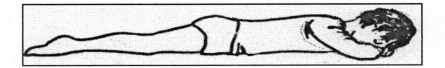

EXERCISE 15: PAWAN MUKTASANA

Lie on your back on the floor.

a) Put arms close to the sides with palms facing up. Breathe in. Start bending legs and pulling knees up towards chest. At the same time, lift head toward the knees while breathing out. Hold.

   Breathe in while extending the legs to a 45 degrees angle to the floor. Hold. Lower the legs while breathing out and relax. Repeat 3-5 times.

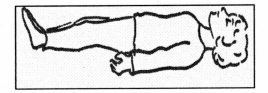

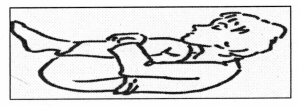

b) "To aid digestion", lie on back.
   Bend the legs so they are perpendicular to the floor and heels are touching hips (or as close as possible), head turned to left, left arm extended to the side of the body with palm up. With fingers of the right hand, form a "knot" and place on the center of the stomach, then concentrate on the stomach. Breathe normally.

   BENEFITS: helps remove constipation and gaseous accumulation in the stomach. Also improves digestion.

EXERCISE 16: YOGA-MUDRA

Sit in Lotus Posture or Easy Posture.
Place your hands behind your body and catch hold of one wrist with the other hand. Lean forward and bend down to touch the floor with your forehead (as best as you can). Breathe normally. Stay relaxed for 30-60 seconds, repeat twice.

BENEFITS: Relieves mental tension. Helps to relax the body and the mind. Removes stiffness from the knees, spine and neck.

MEDITATION

EXERCISE 17: SAVASANA (Dead Pose)

Lie flat in the pose of "corpse". Ultimately, no activity of arms and legs- a completely detached feeling. Lie on back, close eyes, arms away from the body with palms up, feet and legs apart 10"

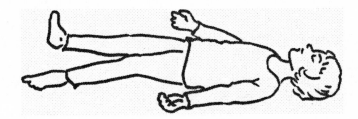

a. Breathe normally and roll your head very gently from side to side. This will help relieve tension in the neck and shoulders, and will help the body relax and clear your mind.

b. "Feel " each part of the body fall off – a sense of being lighter – of floating.

By concentrating on different parts of the body, starting from toes to head, a feeling of relaxation is achieved. Remain totally inactive, effortless and immobile. Ignore all distractions and disturbances. Just focus on your forehead. If your mind wanders off due to noises, thoughts, etc., gently bring it back and focus on your forehead.

With practice, the art of realization will be natural and spontaneous. At that point, the whole body is relaxed to the extent that one forgets the body and the mind achieves alertful rest.

BENEFITS: It is one of the most powerful tools in controlling a large number of diseases caused by tension, high blood pressure, insomnia, etc. This method is very helpful in calming down the mind leading to Meditation.

EXERCISE 18: RELAXING THROUGH MEDITATION

MIND TRIP

Sit in Easy Posture on the floor or sit normally in a straight back chair.

Sit up, close your eyes, clear your mind and focus on the room you are in for 2 minutes.

Then imagine you are walking across a large empty field (no trees, flowers, etc) with a large well with a spiral staircase in the ground in the center of the field. If you feel your mind wandering, concentrate on your mantra or "the" word.

Visualize v-e-r-y slowly going down the well on its spiral staircase. It will get darker and more and more relaxing. If your mind wanders off, slowly bring it back to the well and visualize going down the staircase. Do this for 18 minutes. Don't fall asleep!!! Slowly open your eyes and move your legs.

Reasons to MEDITATE

- ❖ Meditation is a generations old formula that helps unlock the mysteries of mind and paves the way to all-around happiness.
- ❖ Learn how to un-complicate our lives through Meditation.
- ❖ In Meditation, we pay attention to our deepest, inner levels of mind in a quiet and relaxed manner.
- ❖ Meditation is easy to learn-as a matter of fact children as young as five can learn-providing one knows how to work it.
- ❖ Meditation helps us break free of the pain, misery, and bondage caused by frustrating and stressful circumstances.
- ❖ It teaches practical skills to conserve and transform our greatest resource-the energy of our own mind.
- ❖ To end our stress, Meditation provides an easy to use, practical procedure which transforms the dormant powers hidden deep within us.
- ❖ Through regular Meditation the power of the unconscious mind can be transformed into happy, healthy, creative, artistic, productive, loving nurtured and contented lives.
- ❖ In Meditation, one experiences the sixth state of consciousness-above and beyond the everyday stages of consciousness-sleep, wakefulness, dreaming, hypnotic,
- ❖ In Meditation, we are observing and fully alert, yet the mind is not thinking. This is the least excited state of mind.
- ❖ The joy of Meditation is self-reinforcing as in it are utilized the natural tendencies of our mind-we let go the propensity of our mind to think, analyze, remember, and simultaneously enjoy the least excited state of mind.
- ❖ Meditation helps the mind to slow down and eventually stay still-devoid of thoughts and feelings. It replaces the mental activity with an inner awareness and attention.
- ❖ Meditation helps release the tension of the gross and subtle muscles and central nervous system-freeing us from stress.
- ❖ Those who practice Meditation attain a tranquil mind, and this itself adds to our general will-being.
- ❖ After the very first Meditation session, one feels deep rest, increased energy level, determination and creativity.

GETTING
A
GOOD NIGHT'S SLEEP

The ability to fall asleep well is an indication of good health. The body repairs itself through rest resulting from good sleep. Sleep pushes away the bad thoughts from the mind, rests it and prepares it for the challenges of the next day.

The biggest cause of poor sleep is mental anxiety and fear – a negative state of mind.

The obvious answer is to remove that fear and the negative state of mind.

To learn more about getting a good sleep, we will show you simple methods for overcoming the problems of sleeplessness – which, once solved, will lead you to more energy, more productivity and more earning capability.

Good Luck and sleep

well........z.....z.....Z......Z.....Z.....Z.......Z

• • • • • • •

HOW TO FALL ASLEEP IN LESS THAN 30 SECONDS

..........REALLY!!!

Want to feel good, energetic and optimistic?
Get a goodnight's sleep.

Want to be more creative, productive and more efficient?
Get a good night's sleep.

Unfortunately, millions of people suffer from bad sleeping habits, insufficient sleep and no sleep at all (i.e. insomnia). People get into bed start worrying about things (imaginary or nonexistent) toss and turn the whole night and wake up in the morning tired and fatigued.

They drag themselves through the day, feel non-productive or non-creative then pass the day doing injustice to themselves trying to perform their duties, often inefficiently, and thus turning in a lackluster performance. To work late at night and not to give enough rest to the body plays havoc with both the body and the mind. As things get out of hand, the sufferers turn to sedatives, sleeping pills and barbiturates. What stars as simple pill popping to induce sleep slowly turns to addiction? The body then starts to build up resistance to lower dosage and before the user knows it, he is using larger and larger quantities of pills.

Continued use of pills results in lethargy, low productivity, depression and overall slowness of physical movements. Studies have shown that the biggest cause of poor sleep I mental anxiety and fear... a negative state of mind.

Analysis of cases concerning people who complain about the inability to sleep well shows that in most cases, it was fear of something quite specific in their subconscious that caused the problem.

The obvious answer would be to remove this fear. Once the fear is removed, the afflicted people felt relieved, gained confidence and were able to sleep again.

Apart from fear itself, there a re other psychic causes of insomnia, e.g. tension, guilt complex, mental disorientation, anxiety and the inability to face up to the responsibilities of life. All are related to, and caused by the mind and its negative autosuggestions. Modern drugs ma produce relief so that the patient's condition improves temporarily, however, as long as the patient's mental attitude is negative, the improvements cannot remain permanent.

The surest way to combat the cause of illness of psychic origin is through the process of positive identification with oneself.

In order to preserve good health, we must know how to breathe properly and relax completely, both physically and mentally. The practice of Yoga Asana (posture), proper breathing and meditation, along with a well- balanced diet, can help us achieve that.

Experience has shown that regular practice of Yoga Asanas, breathing exercises and Meditation helps to develop harmonious disposition of the consciousness resulting in positive mental approach.

For sound and deep sleep, the following points are recommended:

1. The bedroom should be clean, airy and non-smelly.

2. The bed should be clean and comfortable.

3. The bed should be hard and firm so that the back stays straight and firm. This results in good blood circulation throughout the body

4. The face should not be covered with the sheet or blanket. Breath only through the nose so that clean air goes into the lungs.

5. Sleep on a light stomach. Do not eat a heavy meal just before going to bed.

6. If your feet are cold, warm them up in hot water before getting into bed

7. The mind should be calm and free of worry before you go to sleep. Some light entertainment, like watching a good TV program helps relieve tension resulting in a sound sleep.

8. Wash your face and sprinkle your eyes. Relax through light reading, Meditation or Yoga exercises.

9. Deep breathing exercises for 10-15 minutes before sleeping calms the mind resulting in a sound sleep.

10. Before sleeping, alight massage around the eyes relieves tension

11. Occasionally, lightly massaging the head and scalp will relieve tension.

12. Drink a glass of cold water before sleeping.
13. Sleep in loose clothing

14. If necessary, use a thin pillow.... Although, it is preferable to sleep without one.

Adults should sleep about 8 hours a night. For people over 50 years old, a sleep of 6 hours is often enough. However, deep sleep for 4 hours can refresh the mind and body.

The vitality and well being of the body depends on sound, deep and undisturbed sleep.

z...z...z...z...z...z...z...z...z. **Good night , one and all.**

What Happens During a Laughter Therapy Session?

Breathing Exercises

The session starts with deep breathing exercise, which is done 5 times. People take a deep breath, simultaneously raising their hands up towards the sky, keeping elbows straight. The breath is held for a few seconds while stretching the body.

The breath is then released slowly taking double the time than that of inhalation. This breathing exercise resembles *pranayam* or *tadasna* in yoga.

All the members start chanting ho-ho, ha-ha, with their hands slightly raised and bent at the elbows. The sound should come from deep within the stomach and the mouth should be half open. It is better to do this exercise rhythmically, swinging the body as if one is enjoying the exercise.

Slowly, the speed of the Ho-Ho, Ha-Ha is increased, under the guidance of the anchor- person, who bursts into loud laughter with arms thrown up towards the sky. All the group members follow suit and laughter continues for about 10-15 seconds or more, depending upon the capacity of the individual.

Big or Hearty Laughter

Another kind of laughter, called Big Laughter is initiated with the anchorperson's command 1…2…3… After this laughter, one deep breath is taken just to relax and have a break.

Silent Laughter with Mouth Wide Open

In this laughter, the mouth is opened as wide as possible and participants laugh, making any sound while looking at each other's faces. One can make gestures like showing palms to each other.

Caution: One should not exert too much force while laughing silently. Try to avoid over straining as much as possible.

Humming Laughter with Lips Closed

In this type of laughter, the lips are closed and a person tries to laugh making a little humming sound. This is an excellent exercise for lungs and abdominal muscles, along with all the internal organs.

Medium Laughter

This laughter is the most comfortable and relaxing. It is neither silent, nor is the sound very loud. People greet each other with laughter.

THINK HAPPY : THINK NEUTRAL

Neck & Shoulder Exercises

Since there is some fatigue after completion of the first round, members need to take a break before starting the second round. Here, neck and shoulder exercises are done. They have been incorporated because cervical spondlylosis, neck stiffness, and frozen shoulder are the most common complaints after the age of forty.

Important: Each exercise break should not be for more than FIVE MINUTES. Some laughter clubs try to increase the duration of exercises thereby cutting down the time of laughter. A longer break between the two rounds dampens the enthusiasm for laughter. If desired by the majority of members, any kind of exercises can be conducted after the completion of 15-20 minutes of laughter.

After the five minute exercise break, the group goes for a second laughter session starting with hearty laughter followed by silent, medium and dancing laughter. In between deep breathing exercises are done as in the first round.

When in your daily life, you meet someone too weak to smile, give him yours. Because no one needs a smile more than the person who cannot smile himself.   ...Dale Carnegie

Hasyayog
the Yogic Technique of Laughter

Today, life is very stressful and stress-related diseases are on the rise. 70% of illnesses have some relation to stress. High blood pressure, anxiety, depression, nervous breakdowns, heart disease, peptic ulcers and others, are some of the examples of stress-related diseases.

People use a number of relaxation techniques like yoga, meditation and massage, but the kind of complete relaxation and feeling of joy that you experience while laughing is unique and unparalleled, as it harmonizes all your sense organs in a moment of total concentration. The demands and stressful impact of the modern, mechanized life style is such that people seem to have forgotten to laugh. We have fewer reasons to laugh and many more to feel despondent about.

Basic Research/Yoga Techniques

1. The biggest hurdles, preventing one from laughing are inhibition and shyness. To remove these, the group members are told to gather in large numbers. The larger the group, the easier it is to laugh. Laughter initiated in a large group is contagious and people start laughing, looking at each other's faces.

2. Every member would raise his hand up towards the sky while laughing, which is an easier posture for laughing and makes one feel less inhibited. Each laughing session starts with deep breathing exercise. Members stretch their hands upwards and take deep breaths, hold it for some time and then gradually exhaling. This breathing exercise is similar to '*Pranayam*' in Yoga, which helps in increasing the vital capacity of lungs and helps in producing laughter.

3. After deep breathing, everybody starts chanting Ho-Ho, Ha-Ha. Slowly increasing the speed of Ho-Ho, Ha, Ha, then suddenly burst into hearty laughter by stretching their hand up and looking at each other's faces. Each laughter lasts for about 20-30 seconds and sometimes 45 seconds. This Ho-Ho, Ha-Ha, exercise is akin to yogic exercise call '*Kapalhhati*' where there is a rhythmic movement of the diaphragm and abdominal muscles. It helps to facilitate the lungs in order to initiate laughter. When a large number of people gather in a group and chant Ho-Ho, Ha-Ha, it charges the whole atmosphere with laughter. Since everyone can easily participate in this exercise, each one feels a sense of achievement. This is another step towards removing their inhibitions.

4. All the members were instructed to laugh at the same time following the instructions of an anchorperson that conducted the session. The anchorperson gave his command 1...2...3. If all the members start laughing at the same time, the effect is good. While laughing, participants are instructed to look at each other's faces, as everyone has a peculiar style of laughing. This helps to enhance the stimulus and generate natural laughter.

5. Over a period of 15 days a few more types of laughter's are added like laughing with the mouth wide open, no-sound, laughing with lips closed and little humming sound, medium laughter and cocktail laughter where every member tries laughter in five different ways, like Ha-ha, Ho-ho, Hee-hee, Ooh, Ooh etc. In a nutshell, it is not at all difficult to laugh without jokes if laughter is practiced in a group.

You must be able to handle tension-not let it manhandle you. Relax!
Calm down, stop rushing around and take hold of your life
.... George Shinn

LAUGH AND BE HEALTHY

What is laughter, after all? It is a reflex that sets your diaphragm going. It makes your respiratory muscles rapidly expand and contract, enhancing your breathing apparatus and revving up your circulation. The expansion and contraction increases the chest cavity and the lungs inhale more oxygen while simultaneously expelling more carbon dioxide.

As soon as this happens, a chain reaction is triggered off in your body, say fitness and health experts. It produces adrenalin, the 'arousal hormone' that awakens your senses. Simultaneously, your heartbeats quicken and you pupils dilate.

Due to this positive stress on your heart, the heart pumps a greater dose of blood through your arteries and draws in more of it through your veins. That is why your face gets flushed.

Moreover, the adrenalin thus activated, causes your pituitary glands to release ACTH (adrenocorticotropic hormone) which, in turn, stimulates the adrenal cortex to secrete cortisol. This has anti-inflammatory properties and is especially useful for people suffering from arthritis.

While not yet conclusive, more and more medical experts are beginning to believe that laughter also releases endorphine-the body's natural painkiller.

Many sources of happiness

If laughter is the voice of good humor, a smile is the expression of happiness-the very foundation of a healthy life. In his book, *Psychology of Happiness*, Michael Fordyce writes, "Happy individuals live a balanced life, so they have many sources of happiness. When happiness depends on one thing, you are on shaky ground."

Indeed, happiness is at its most brittle when its cause is a one-pointed material possession. Those who felt the thrill vanish after acquiring a new microwave oven, would know what the phrase "there is more fun in the anticipation than in the acquisition" means. Fordyce's suggestion makes sense in this context. Broad base your foundations and you can live happily ever after in the house called happiness. And a smile really goes a long mile towards that destination.

Says Dr Kataria, "Laughing silently with your mouth closed is akin to blowing a balloon. It is especially good for asthma and bronchitis, the 2 common ailments. Similarly laughing silently with an open mouth is good for older people with chest infections.

Interestingly, laughter is being seen as a stress-releaser everywhere. "Watch a sitcom and de-stress your self" is a common catch phrase.

Psychiatrists are also urging their depressed patients to simulate a smile when the real thing vanishes in the blues. The mere movement of those minor muscles of the mouth set in a smile, relieve you tension. And it isn't long before the real thing occupies its place!

Many people are notorious for their 'giggles'!… Why not use them for enhancing your health? Start a laughing club in your society or neighborhood. You can even start with a small group of 5 as Dr. Kataria did.

Laughter is infectious

Initially, you may feel a little self-conscious. But, it is not as silly as it sounds. The muscles of you mouth quiver in a self-deprecatory smirk, your nerves twitch, your lips droop like an inverted crescent moon.

Then, you catch your neighbors eye. And suddenly, it strikes you. The giggle becomes full-throated rumble. "Ho-ho, ha-ha!" you chorus. Others will join in. For laughter is infectious. At the end of it, you can ask, "There, it wasn't so difficult, was it?" And chuckle some more!

To conclude, laughter can act as an illness preventor-depressed people are more prone to sickness than those with a sunny disposition. So, work on your funny bone. For, often that is all you need-a good hearty laugh to brighten up your day!

Never under-estimate yourself. You are the most important thing in the universe   ………. Edward L. Kramer

Health Benefits of Laughter Therapy

Most Important: People suffering from a variety of diseases have benefited in some way or the other. But we don't claim to have cured long-standing ailments with laughter therapy. Laughter is more of a supplementary and preventive therapy.

Sense of Well Being

The one benefit everybody gets is a sense of well-being. After 15 minutes of laughter in the morning you will feel fresh throughout the day.

There is no medicine like laughter therapy, which gives you instant results. You start feeling the freshness straightaway. Many people have found that they don't get irritated over trivial things after starting this therapy. Their approach towards life changes positively.

Depression, anxiety, and psychosomatic disorders, the stress and strain of modern life are taking a heavy toll on the human mind. Mind related diseases like anxiety, depression, nervous breakdown, and sleeplessness are on the rise. Laughter has benefited many people who were on heavy tranquilizers and sleeping pills. Now they are getting better sleep and their depression has reduced.

Meditation and Relaxation

Laughter Therapy is one of the finest anti-stress measures. It is ideally suited for today's stress ridden lifestyle. It can be compared to any form of meditation or relaxation. To achieve the desired end through Meditation, one has to put in a concerted effort to completely detach oneself on mental and emotional levels from one's own feelings and thought process, as well as from the physical world to prevent distractions. On the other hand, while laughing, we do not have any conscious thought process and all our senses naturally and effortlessly combine in a moment of harmony, to give joy, peace, and relaxation.

In other types of meditation you need to concentrate a lot to take your mind away from distraction thoughts, which is easier said than done. Therefore, Laughter Therapy is the easiest form of meditation, a form that brings you instant relaxation.

High Blood Pressure and Heart Disease

There are a number of causes for high blood pressure and heart disease, like hereditary, being overweight, smoking and excessive intake of saturated fats. But stress is one of the most important factors.

Laughter definitely helps to control blood pressure by reducing the release of stress related hormones and bringing relaxation. In experiments it has been noticed that there is a drop of 10-20 mm pressure after participation for 10 minutes in a laughter session. It does not mean that those who are taking 2-3 tablets for blood pressure everyday will be completely cured. Maybe you will require 2 tablets if you are taking 3 or borderline high blood pressure patients may not require any medication.

It takes years to develop high blood pressure; it cannot be reversed in a few days or a month. But definitely laughter will exercise some control and arrest further progress of the disease.

Similarly, if you are at a high risk of developing heart disease laughter may be the best preventive medicine. Those who are suffering from heart disease and have stabilized on medication will find laughter therapy improves the blood circulation and oxygen levels to the heart muscles. Those who have had heart attacks or have undergone bypass surgery can also participate in laughter therapy.

Strengthens the Immune System

Our immune system plays a most important role in keeping good health or development of infections, allergies, and cancer.

It has been noted by psycho-neuroimmunologists that all negative emotions like anxiety, depression, or anger weaken the immune system of the body, thereby reducing its fighting capacity against infections. Laughter helps to increase the count of natural killer lymphocytes (a type of white cell) and also raises the antibody levels.

Researchers have found more antibodies in the mucous of the nose and respiratory passages after laughter therapy. There are many members of laughter clubs who have noticed that the frequency of common colds, sore throats, and chest infections has reduced.

Bronchitis and Asthma

Laughter is one of the best exercises for those suffering from asthma and bronchitis. It improves the lung capacity and oxygen levels in the blood. Doctors recommend chest physiotherapy to bring out mucous (phlegm) from the respiratory passages. Blowing forcefully into an instrument and blowing balloons is one of the common exercises given to asthmatics. Laughter therapy does the same job, more easily and cheaply.

There are many individuals suffering from asthma and bronchitis who participate in laughter clubs. They have reported reduced frequency of their attacks. Laughter therapy may cause some discomfort if you have severe bronchspasm. There are a small percentage of asthma cases that may get a little aggravation by doing any exercise (exercise induced asthma). Such individuals should consult their doctors before taking up laughter therapy.

One of the most common causes for frequent attacks of asthma is infection. Laughter therapy increases the antibody levels in the mucous membrane of the respiratory passages, thereby reducing the frequency of chest infections. It also tones up the normal mucous clearing system of the bronchial tubes. Stress is another factor, which, can bring on an attack of asthma. By reducing stress, it might improve the prognosis of the disease.

Internal Jogging

There are plenty of exercises available for your body muscles, but laughing provides a good massage to all internal organs. It has been compared to magic fingers which reach into the interior of the abdomen and massage your organs.

Good for Actors and Singers

Laughter therapy can be very beneficial for singers and actors. Increased lung capacity, exercise of the diaphragm and abdominal muscles will help to gain a better control over speech. It may enhance self confidence and reduce stage fright.

Makes You Look Younger

People do exercise for all the muscles of the body, but there is no regular exercise designed for facial muscles except in Yoga. Laughter is an excellent exercise for your facial muscles. It tones up the muscles of the face and improves facial expressions. When you laugh, your face becomes red due to an increase in blood supply which nourishes the facial skin and makes it glow.

Laughing people look more cheerful and attractive. By squeezing the tear glands through laughter, it moistens the eyes adding a little sparkle to them. Laughter exercises your abdominal muscles and helps to improve muscle tone of those with pot bellies.

Self Confidence through Laughter

When you are laughing in a group at a public place with your arms up towards the sky, it removes your inhibitions and over a period of time you become a more sociable, unreserved and outgoing person. Admittedly, some people are a bit reluctant to join the laughter group initially, in spite of strong inclinations for it, for fear of appearing absurd to onlookers. However, this is a passing phase and the very decision to join a laughter club opens you mind. Gradually, it also adds to your self confidence.

It will also help to develop you personality and leadership qualities. In a laughter club, many members are encouraged to conduct the session. People, who were not able to speak a word in public, often become very good public speakers. With the passage of time, you will observe a transformation in your personality. You develop a more positive attitude towards life. Minor setbacks or irritants in every day life no longer cause a serious disturbance, and you learn to deal with them much more effectively.

Don't permit yourself to show temper. Always remember that if you are right you can afford to keep your temper, and if you are wrong you cannot afford to lose it.
.... J.J.Reynolds

Laughter Therapy's Possible Benefits to Children are:

1. Laughter therapy will increase the level of relaxation and reduce nervousness and stage fright.
2. It will help children to be more outgoing and develop self-confidence.
3. Laughter therapy will increase their stamina and breathing capacity enabling them to excel in sports activities.
4. Laughter therapy will increase oxygen supply and improve mental functions and academic performance.
5. Cheerful moods will become a way of life and help children to develop a positive attitude towards life as well as enhance their leadership qualities.

We are approaching educational authorities and Government officials to introduce Laughter Therapy in schools and colleges. Meanwhile, we shall also assist and guide people who wish to start Laughter Clubs in private schools or colleges.

Laughter Therapy in Corporate Houses

In Japan, it used to be a regular practice to do some physical exercises in office premises in the morning before employees start their work. All the members of the company at all levels participate.

We believe that introducing Laughter Therapy in corporate houses is a very significant and worthwhile idea. It can help to improve inter-personal relationships at all levels in an organization, replacing mutual lack of trust and confidence with a more positive outlook and cooperative attitude towards one's colleagues and subordinates. This should in turn definitely help to improve the prevalent work environment and overall performance of an organization.

Who Should Not Join a Laughing Club?

People are instructed to laugh forcefully so that all the residual air in the lungs is emptied and is replaced by oxygen-rich fresh air. Forceful laughter involves some physical strain and rise in abdominal pressure. Patients with the following complications are those who should not join in laughter therapy sessions.

Hernia: Hernia is a protrusion of the abdominal contents through the muscle wall of the abdominal cavity. Those suffering from inguinal (groin) hernia or abdominal incisional (operative scar) hernia should avoid attending laughter sessions. This is because laughter produces additional abdominal pressure and may aggravate the condition. However, if the patient has undergone surgical treatment for hernia, he/she could be assessed by a surgeon for fitness before attending laughter therapy.

Advanced Piles: The condition of patients with long standing piles may worsen with laughter therapy. They should get themselves treated before attending therapy.

Heart Disease with Chest Pain: Heart Patients who get chest pain while walking or during routine activity, should not participate. Patients whose condition has stabilized and who can walk for 30-45 minutes without difficulty, are fit to join the laughing session. Avoid laughter therapy for three months after a heart attack and two months following abdominal surgery.

Prolapse: Ligaments supporting the uterus become weak after the age of 40. They may sag and cause prolapse of the uterus. Such women have lover abdominal discomfort and may lose complete control over their urine flow (stress incontinence). They should avoid laughter therapy until they are treated surgically.

Pregnancy: Pregnant women may undergo an abortion if there is a rise in abdominal pressure and hence should avoid attending a laughter session. Even patients without any illness, but who feel uneasy after a laughter session should discontinue their attendance and consult a doctor.

Severe Cold and Flu: Those suffering from a viral common cold with running nose along with fever and chest infection should stay away from the group for 2-3 days until the infection and fever settle down.

ACKNOWLEDGEMENTS

1. Yogacharaya Mahavir Sainik :PremPuri Adhyatma
2. Yogasana & Sadhna
   Bhartiya Yoga Sansthan
3. Dr. Satyapal & Dr. D. D. Agarwal Yoga (1977) –
   Vivekananda Kendra
4. Simple Yoga – Mr. T. P. Sreekumaran
   Yoga Brotherhood (Regd),
5. Priyadarshini Laughing Club International
6. Women's Era (Shalan Savur)
7. The Holy Geeta – Commentry by Chinmayananda

ABOUT THE AUTHOR

Sushil Bhatia has been a student of Yoga and Meditation since he was a young business owner in New Delhi, India. Throughout the years, he has periodically taught Yoga and Meditation and has formed the practice as an integral part of his everyday life.

And a busy life it is. With a Ph.D in physical chemistry, an MBA and several other degrees, he has owned a manufacturing plant in New Delhi, India and worked all over the world for Dennison Manufacturing Company (he speaks three languages fluently). He presently is the President of JMD Manufacturing Inc. in Framingham, Massachusetts, U.S.A.

Sushil invents. Innovation is a way of life for him. Professionally, he has developed, a glue stick, electro sensitive paper, a cold seal packaging protection for electronic goods and, most recently, a decopier process that removes ink from copy paper without damaging the original. For that, he was a finalist in 1998 in a national inventors competition sponsored by Discover magazine.

So, ideas flow constantly. His interest in Yoga and Meditation and Laughter Therapy somehow merged with his remarkable sense of humor and positive attitude, hence the formulation of the Laughing clubs of America (the idea came from the existence of Laughing clubs of India). By merging the benefits of laughter with the practice of Yoga and Meditation, a lot of people are already living more healthy and relaxed lives and are more easily coping with the stresses of daily living.

Sushil lives with his wife and children in Framingham.

They laugh a lot.

COME   LAUGH   WITH US

Printed in the United States
29521LVS00002B/76-126